On Our Plate!

Featuring

StoryWalk Authors

Audrey Andrews

Megan Cline

Karen Graves

Heather Nelson

Lee Shaw

Kristy Stephens

and

Storywalk Illustrators

Brie Riley

Nikita Seledkov

These are works of fiction. All of the characters, organizations and events portrayed in this novel are either products of the authors' imagination or used fictionally.

On Our Plate!

Copyright © 2015 by Oregon State University Extension Clackamas County

All rights reserved. No part of this book may be used or reproduced in any manner whatsoever without written permission except in the case of brief quotations embodied in critical articles or reviews. For information address OSU Extension Clackamas County Family and Community Health, 200 Warner Milne Road, Oregon City, OR 97045.

Printed in the United States of America

Paperback Edition / July 2015

Funding for the Molalla Storywalk provided by the Moore Family Center-Healthy Community Outreach Project Statewide Initiative.

In Collaboration with GROW (Generating Rural Options for Weight) Healthy Kids and Communities, Let's Move! Molalla, City of Molalla, Molalla Public Library, Molalla River School District, Molalla Area Chamber of Commerce, and local businesses of the Molalla area

One day, a little boy named Toby felt his tummy rumbling. He decided to go on an adventure to find some of the healthiest foods in the solar system. He kissed his mom goodbye and sprung out the door.

On the first day, Toby marched to Mercury.

There he did one handstand and felt happy. Then he ate a serving of amaranth porridge and an apple.

Un día , un niño que se llamaba Toby sintió que su estómago estaba haciendo unos ruidos extraños. Decidió salir en una aventura para buscar las comidas más saludables en el sistema solar. Le dio un beso de despedida a su mamá, y salió disparado por la puerta.

El primer día, Toby se marchó a Mercurio.

Allá, hizo un paro de manos y se sintió feliz. Comió una porción de atole de amaranto y una manzana.

On the second day, he vaulted to Venus.

There he did two push-ups and felt powerful. Then he ate a bowl of chard salad with chia.

On the third day, Toby moonwalked to Mars.

El segundo día, voló a Venus.

Allá, hizo dos planchas y se sintió poderoso. Comió un plato de ensalada de acelgas con semillas de chía.

El tercer día, Toby hizo la danza de "moonwalk" para ir a Marte.

There he did three sit-ups and felt satisfied. Then he ate a bowl of farro stew and fennel.
On the fourth day, Toby jumped to Jupiter.

Allá, hizo tres abdominales y se sintió satisfecho. Comió un plato de guisado de farro e hinojo.
El cuarto día, Toby viajó a Júpiter.

There he did four cartwheels and felt confident. Then he ate Kamut soup with kale.
On the fifth day, Toby skipped to Saturn.

Allá, hizo cuatro piruetas y se sintió lleno de confianza. Comió una sopa de Kamut con col rizada.
El quinto día, Toby saltó a Saturno.

There he did five jumping jacks and felt joyful. Then he ate a bowl of cooked millet and melon.
On the sixth day, Toby unicycled to Uranus.

Allá, hizo cinco saltos de tijera y se sintió alegre. Comió un plato de millo cocido y melón.
El sexto día, Toby se montó en un monociclo para ir a Urano.

There he did six arm circles and felt awesome. Then he ate hot quinoa with carrots.
On the seventh day, Toby noodled to Neptune.

Allá, hizo seis giros de los brazos y se sintió genial. Entonces comió quínoa caliente con zanahorias.
El séptimo día, Toby navegó a Neptuno.

There he did seven frog hops and felt fulfilled. Then he ate a serving of popped sorghum with snap peas.
On the eighth day, Toby pogoed to the dwarf planet Pluto.

Allá, hizo siete saltos de rana y se sintió realizado. Comió una porción de sorgo con los chícharos.
El octavo día, Toby salió dando brincos con su palo saltador hacia el pequeñito planeta Plutón.

There he did eighth chinups and felt cheerful. Then he ate spelt spaghetti with sauce.
On the ninth day, Toby returned to Earth.

Allá, se elevó ocho veces en una barra fija y se sintió entusiasmado. Comió espagueti de espelta con salsa.
El noveno día, Toby regresó a la Tierra.

There he did nine toe touches and felt triumphant. Then he ate teff salad and a tangerine.

Allá se tocó los dedos de pie nueve veces y se sintió triunfante. Comió una ensalada de teff y una mandarina.

Toby let out a big yawn and realized how tired he was. So he kissed his mom goodnight, hopped into bed, and drifted off to sleep, where he dreamed of yummy food and fun activities.

Toby bostezó y se dio cuenta de lo cansado que estaba. Le dio un beso de buenas noches a su mamá, y brincó a la cama para dormir, y soñó con comida rica y actividades divertidas.

Ruby's Special Pizza
La Pizza Especial de Ruby

Written by/Escrito por Megan Cline
Illustrated by/Illustrado por Brie Riley

Ruby rides in the shopping cart past the frozen pizzas.

"Mommy, can we have pizza for dinner?"

Mommy pushes her cart past the pizzas. "Yes, but we're going to make a special kind of pizza that doesn't come from a freezer, box or delivery man. Will you be my special helper?"

"Yes," Ruby says. "I'll be your special helper."

Ruby va en el carrito de compras y pasa por enfrente de la pizza congelada.

"¿Mami, podemos cenar pizza?"

Mami dirige el carrito más allá que las pizzas. "Sí, pero vamos a hacer una pizza especial que no viene congelada, ni es de caja, ni es de entrega a domicilio. ¿Vas a ser mi ayudante especial?"

"Sí," dice Ruby. "Voy a ser tu ayudante especial."

Mommy goes through the store for the things they don't have at home. She picks out:

    Shredded low-fat cheese
    Fresh Spinach
    Sliced Mushrooms
    Tomato Sauce

Mami va por la tienda buscando las cosas que no tienen en la casa. Ella recoge:
Queso rallado bajo en grasa
Espinaca fresca
Champiñones en trozos
Salsa de Tomate

At home, Ruby washes her hands and puts on her apron.

Mommy takes spinach, cheese, tomato sauce, and mushrooms out of the grocery bag.

"Where's the flat bread thing we put the cheese on?" Ruby asks.

"We're going to make a special crust for our special pizza," Mommy says.

En la casa, Ruby se lava las manos y se pone su delantal.

Mami saca la espinaca, el queso, la salsa de tomate, y los champiñones de la bolsa. "¿Dónde está el tipo de pan plano para poner el queso?" pregunta Ruby.

"Nosotros vamos a hacer una corteza especial para nuestra pizza especial," dice Mami.

Ruby helps Mommy mix together the ingredients for a crust with whole wheat flour, sugar, salt, yeast, oil and warm water at just the right temperature so the yeast will grow. While they wait for their dough to rise, Mommy gives Ruby a colander and fills it with spinach leaves. She carefully carries it to the sink and runs water over the leaves to clean them and dry them with a clean dish towel.

Ruby ayuda a Mami mezclar todos los ingredientes de la corteza con harina de trigo integral, azúcar, sal, levadura, aceite y agua tibia a la temperatura perfecta para que crezca la levadura. Mientras esperan que crezca la masa, Mami da a Ruby una coladera y lo llena con las hojas de espinaca. Lo lleva con cuidado al fregadero y pasa agua encima de las hojas para limpiarlas, y las seca con una toalla limpia.

"Do we have those red spicy things I like on my pizza?" Ruby asks.

"Pepperoni? No, but I have something even better."

Mommy takes a big piece of chicken leftover from their dinner the night before and cuts it into smaller pieces. As they finish their tasks, the timer beeps.

"Our dough is ready," Mommy says.

"¿Tenemos esas cosas rojas que pican que me gustan en mi pizza?" pregunta Ruby.

"Peperoni? No, pero tengo algo aún mejor."

Mami saca un pedazo de pollo que había preparado para la cena de la noche anterior, y lo corta en pedazos pequeños. Cuando terminan sus tareas, el medidor de tiempo suena.

"Está lista la masa," dice Mami.

Mommy shapes the dough in a circle and carefully places it in a round pan. She spoons sauce on the center and sprinkles a little bit of the cheese on the pizza. "Too much cheese isn't healthy, but just a little will make our pizza taste very good. Now, you can put the spinach on it."

Mami forma la masa en un círculo y la pone con cuidado en un molde redondo. Usa una cuchara para poner la salsa en el medio y rocía la pizza con queso.

"Demasiado queso no es muy saludable, pero un poco le da un buen sabor a nuestra pizza. Ahora, puedes colocar la espinaca."

Ruby covers the crust in green leaves and sprinkles the mushrooms on top, followed by the chicken. Mommy adds one last sprinkle of cheese.

"Now, we're ready to cook it."

Mommy carefully puts the pizza in the oven and sets the timer for twenty minutes.

Ruby cubre la corteza con las hojas verdes y coloca los champiñones encima, y después el pollo. Mami agrega un poco más de queso.

"Ahora, estamos listas para hornearla."

Mami pone la pizza en el horno con cuidado y pone el medidor de tiempo a veinte minutos.

Meanwhile, Ruby sets the table. When the pizza is ready, Mommy sets it on the table along with a tray of vegetables.

"I'll show you how to fix your plate," Mommy says. "Pick out the vegetables you want to eat and fill half your plate with them."

Mientras tanto, Ruby pone la mesa. Cuando está lista la pizza, Mami la pone en la mesa con un plato de verduras.

"Te enseño como preparar tu plato," dice Mami. "Escoge las verduras que quieres comer y llena la mitad de tu plato con ellas."

Ruby fills half her plate with mostly carrots and a few pieces of celery. Mommy then puts two pieces of pizza on Ruby's plate.

Ruby takes a bite of her special pizza. "This is yummy! I like chicken better than those pepperoni things."

Ruby llena la mitad de su plato principalmente con zanahorias y unos cuantos palitos de apio. Mami pone dos pedazos de pizza en el plato de Ruby.

Ruby prueba un bocado de su pizza especial. "¡Está rica! Me gusta más el pollo que esos peperonis."

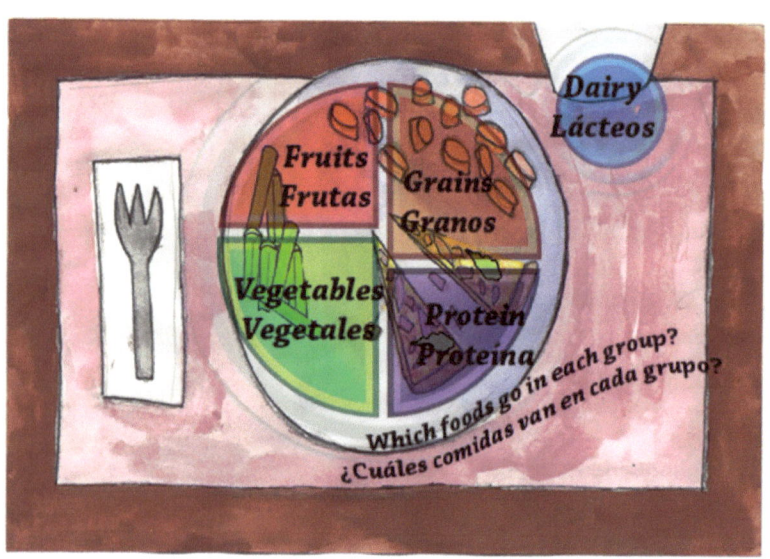

"It's healthy for you too. It has whole grains in the crust, low-fat dairy in the cheese, lean protein in the chicken, and vegetables from the sauce, mushrooms and spinach. You should eat lots of vegetables every day so that's why we have the celery and carrots on the side. For dessert, we'll have apple slices."

"Yummy! But what are we going to do with the leftovers?"

"Además es saludable. Tiene granos integrales en la corteza, lácteos bajos en grasa en el queso, proteína de carne magra en el pollo, y verduras en la salsa, en los champiñones y en las espinacas. Debes de comer muchas verduras cada día y por eso tenemos las zanahorias y el apio al lado. Para el postre, comemos manzana."

"¡Mmm! ¿Pero qué hacemos con las sobras?

At school the next day, Ruby goes to the cafeteria for lunch. She opens the lunchbox Mommy packed with a piece of pizza, a little bag of carrots, an apple, and a bottle of water.

"What's that?" Ruby's friend asks.

"It's the special pizza we had for dinner last night. Mommy and I made it ourselves. Want to know how we did it?"

En la escuela el próximo día, Ruby va a la cafetería para almorzar. Abre la lonchera en la que Mami había empacado un pedazo de pizza, una bolsita de zanahorias, una manzana y una botella de agua.

"¿Qué es eso?" preguntaron los amigos de Ruby.

"Es la pizza especial que comimos en la cena anoche. Mami y yo la hicimos nosotras mismas. ¿Quieren saber cómo la hicimos?"

We like outdoor fun! In parks we learn to play games and be safe. We teeter-totter with our friends. I SPY a Red Roof. Do you?

¡Nos gusta jugar afuera! En los parques aprendemos jugar y estar seguros. Jugamos en el subibaja con nuestros amigos. YO ESPIO un Techo Rojo. ¿Y tú?

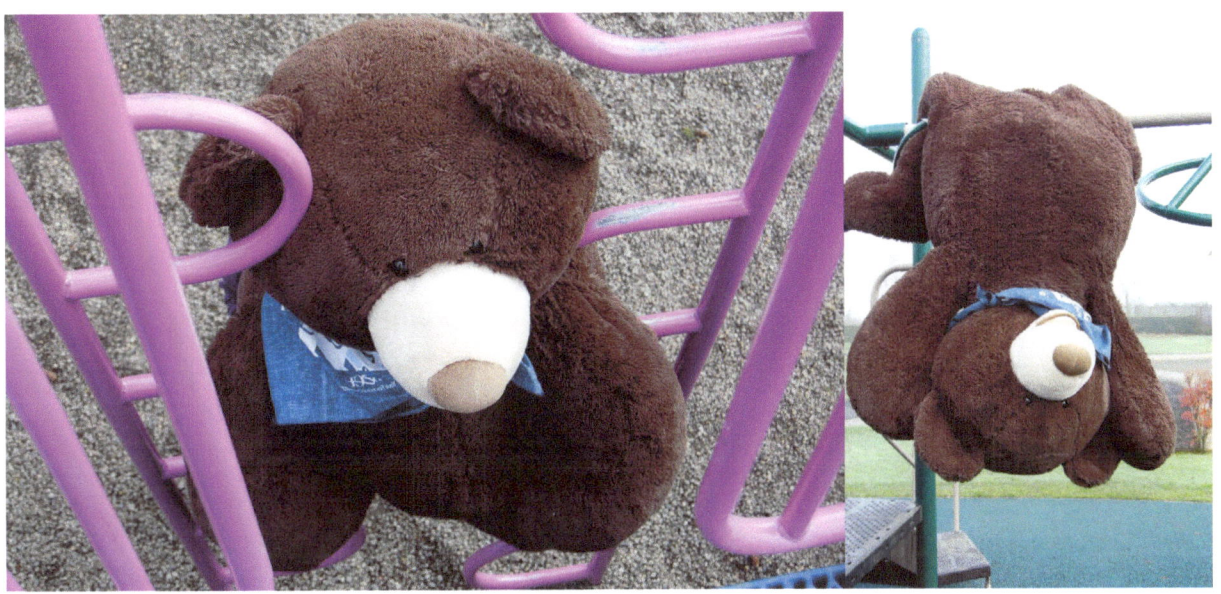

We swing and climb on the bars with our strong legs and strong arms.

Jugamos en los columpios y subimos a las barras con nuestras piernas fuertes y nuestros brazos fuertes.

Give us tasty fruits and vegetables for energy, and we will have power to slide! I SPY a Tasty Apple. Do you?

Danos frutas y verduras para tener energía, y nosotros podremos jugar en el tobogán. YO ESPIO una Manzana Rica. ¿Y tú?

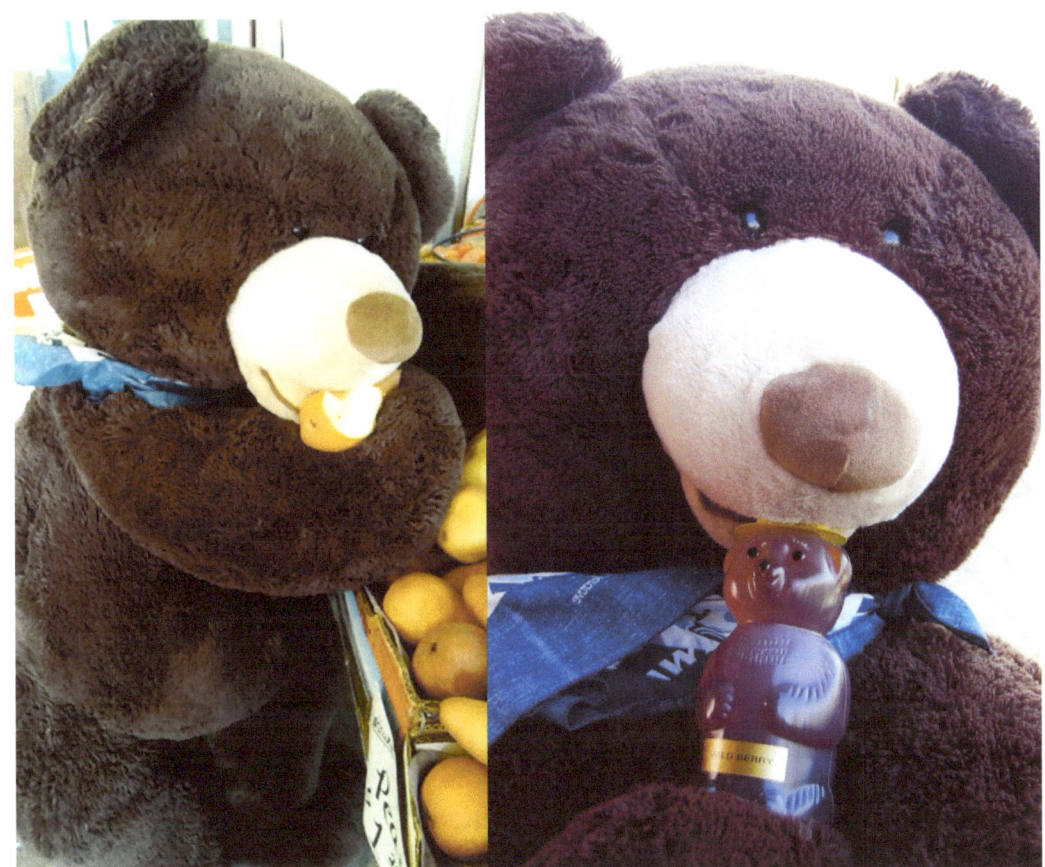

At our picnic, we eat delicious food from all of the food groups,

En nuestro picnic, comemos ricos alimentos de todos los grupos de comida.

And our bodies love water! I SPY Four Bear Ears. Do you?

¡Y a nuestros cuerpos les encanta el agua! YO ESPIO cuatro orejas de oso. ¿Y tú?

Climbing is our favorite adventure, and we have to decide where to put our hands and feet.

Escalar es nuestra aventura favorita, y tenemos que decidir dónde poner las manos y los pies.

We leave the park on our bikes and ride to the Molalla River Corridor. I SPY a Trail. Do you?

Salimos del parque en nuestras bicicletas y vamos al Rio Molalla. YO ESPIO un Sendero. ¿Y tú?

At the river we splash and play! We hike on the trails and find our favorite plants and flowers. I SPY a tree trunk. Do you?

¡En el rio salpicamos y jugamos en el agua! Caminamos en los senderos y encontramos nuestras plantas y flores favoritas. YO ESPIO un tronco de árbol ¿Y tú?

After our adventure, it's time to go home.

Después de nuestra aventura, es hora de regresar a casa.

It is a good day when we can play, eat healthy food, and go to bed with happy dreams.

Es un buen día cuando podemos jugar, comer saludable y acostarnos con sueños felices.

DAISY
The Protector Dog Cares for Her Friends
El Perro Protector Cuida de sus Amigos

Heather L. Nelson

Hi, I'm Daisy. I live on a farm in the mountains. I have lots of room to run and play.

My job is to protect. I check the property and make sure everything is okay on the farm.

Hola, soy Daisy. Vivo en una granja en las montañas. Tengo mucho espacio para correr y jugar.

Mi trabajo es proteger. Reviso el terreno y me aseguro de que todo esté bien en la granja.

I have a little friend named Buddy. I always protect him. I make sure he never gets lost.

Tengo un amiguito que se llama Buddy. Siempre le protejo. Me aseguro de que nunca se pierda.

Sometimes we see birds, chipmunks and other critters. I chase them away.

A veces, vemos aves, ardillas y otras criaturas. Yo las persigo y las ahuyento.

Buddy and I run and play together. Running is good exercise for people and dogs. It makes us both stronger.

Buddy y yo corremos y jugamos juntos. Correr es un buen ejercicio para las personas y para los perros. Nos hace más fuertes a los dos.

I tell Buddy to eat healthy food to help him grow strong. He likes carrots and I like carrots! If he wants to share with me, I will help him eat his carrot. Some foods, like carrots, are good for dogs and people. Yum, that was good!

Le digo a Buddy que debe comer comida saludable para ayudarle a crecer fuerte. ¡A él le gustan las zanahorias y a mí me gustan las zanahorias! Si quiere compartir conmigo, le ayudaré comer su zanahoria. Algunas comidas, como las zanahorias, son buenas para los perros y para los humanos. ¡Mm, estuvo muy rico!

I have a little dog friend named Peanut. I really like Peanut. Peanut likes to play with me, but she has short legs and can't run as fast as I do. I have long legs and could keep running very fast, but I always slow down and wait for her to catch up.

Tengo una perrita que es mi amiga que se llama Peanut. Me agrada mucho Peanut. A Peanut le gusta jugar conmigo, pero tiene las piernas cortas y no puede correr tan rápido. Yo tengo las piernas largas y puedo correr muy rápido, pero siempre me paro y espero para que me alcance ella.

Sometimes, Buddy carries Peanut when she gets tired. Peanut doesn't get exercise when she is carried, but I guess Buddy gets more exercise!

A veces, Buddy carga a Peanut cuando ella se cansa. Peanut no está haciendo ejercicio cuando la carga, ¡pero supongo que Buddy esté haciendo más ejercicio!

I tell Peanut to eat healthy food. It will give her strength to run faster.

Le digo a Peanut que debe comer comida saludable. Le dará fuerza para correr más rápido.

I tell Peanut to get lots of rest, because that will also help her have more energy when she is outside playing.

Le digo a Peanut que debe descansar bastante, porque eso le ayudará tener más energía cuando ella esté jugando afuera.

I tell Peanut and Buddy to drink a lot of water. Water is good for people and dogs. It will help them be healthy. We all need to drink lots of water. Besides, water tastes really good!

Les digo a Peanut y a Buddy que deben tomar mucha agua. El agua es buena para las personas y para los perros. Les ayuda estar saludables. Todos nosotros necesitamos tomar mucha agua. ¡Además, el agua sabe muy rico!

I really like my job to protect my farm and my friends. I like to make sure everything and everyone is safe.

Me encanta mi trabajo de proteger mi granja y a mis amigos. Me gusta asegurarme que todo el mundo esté seguro.

I care for my friends Buddy and Peanut. I want to help them be healthy. When we run and play together, we all have fun and we all stay healthy!

Cuido a mis amigos Buddy y Peanut. Quiero ayudarles a ser saludables. ¡Cuando corremos y jugamos juntos, nos divertimos todos y nos mantenemos saludables!

Jack and the Beans
Jack y los Ejotes

L. Lee Shaw

"I hate green beans." Jack glared at the pile sitting on his plate.

"That's not very nice," his mother said. "Grandma worked hard to grow those beans for us to enjoy."

"And not just me," Grandma said. "I have a whole team of workers that helped those beans grow. Maybe you would like to meet them?"

"Odio los ejotes." Jack miró con furia al montón de ejotes en su plato.

"Mijo, eso no es muy amable," dijo su madre. "Tu abuela trabajaba duro para cultivar esos ejotes para que nosotros los podamos disfrutar.

"Y no solo yo," dijo la Abuela. "Tengo un equipo entero de trabajadores que me ayudan a cultivar esos ejotes. ¿Quizás los quisieras conocer?

In the garden, Grandma pulled a magnifying glass out of her pocket and handed it to Jack. "Here, you will need this. Now look very carefully there." **She pointed to a place by her bean plants.**

"I don't see anything."

"Look closer."

En el huerto, la Abuela sacó una lupa de su bolsillo y se la dio a Jack. "Aquí tienes, la vas a necesitar. Ahora, mira con cuidado allá." Ella señaló hacia un sitio al lado de las plantas de ejotes.

"No veo nada."

"Acércate."

Suddenly, a worm dressed as a cowboy appeared. "Howdy, pardner!" said the worm, twirling a lasso over his head. "I'm Clod, the best worm wrangler in this here garden."

"Worm wrangler?" Jack said.

"Yup. Worms wriggle through the soil, loosening it up so seeds have a soft place to do their growing. Can't put down roots or send up shoots if the ground is hard."

De repente, apareció un gusano disfrazado como un vaquero. "¿Qué onda, amigo?" dijo el gusano, girando un lazo encima de su cabeza. "Soy Clod, el mejor gusano vaquero en este huerto."

"Gusano vaquero?" dijo Jack.

"Sí, hombre. Los gusanos se mueven por la tierra, aflojándola para que las semillas tengan un espacio suave para crecer. No pueden echar raíces ni tener brotes si la tierra está dura."

"Worms are real important livestock, but, dagnab it, if you don't watch them, they start heading off in every direction. Next thing you know they plumb forgot about the beans and are helping out a dandelion. Then it's my job to round them up and get them back into the garden. The Seed Nanny gets pretty mad if she doesn't have nice, soft beds for her babies."

"Los gusanos son animales importantes, pero carambas, si no los miras, empiezan a caminar por todos lados. De repente se olvidan de los ejotes y ayudan a crecer a los dientes de león. Entonces es mi trabajo juntarlos y devolverlos al huerto. La Nana de Semillas se enoja si no tiene camas bien suaves para sus bebés."

"Seed Nanny?"
"Move the magnifying glass a little this way," piped a voice. When Jack did, he saw a plump seed wearing an apron.

"¿Nana de Semillas?"
"Mueve la lupa por aquí un poco." Dijo una voz. Cuando lo hizo Jack, vio a una semilla rolliza llevando un delantal.

"Hi, Jack, I'm the Seed Nanny and I take over after your grandma tucks those bean seeds into the earth. It's my job to make sure they are taken care of until it's time for them to sprout."

"Hola, Jack, yo soy la Nana de Semillas y estoy a cargo de las semillas de ejotes después de que tu abuela las arropara en la tierra. Es mi trabajo cuidarlas hasta que llegue el momento de brotar."

"They don't do it themselves?" Jack asked

"Oh my, no. They kick their dirt off and have to be tucked in again. They get to wiggling and next thing you know they've got their roots poking out of the ground and their shoots heading down. It's a lot of work getting those seeds to grow up proper."

"¿No lo hacen ellas solitas?" preguntó Jack.

"Ay, no. Patean la tierra y las tengo que arropar otra vez. Se empiezan a mover y pronto tienen sus raíces arriba de la tierra y sus brotes para abajo. Es mucho trabajo cuidar a las semillas para que crezcan bien."

Just then a sweet voice spoke to Jack. "Hello, Jack. I see you have met my assistants."

Jack looked through the magnifying glass trying to find the new voice. "Oh, Jack, you are already looking at me. I am the earth, and the air; the sun and the rain. I am Mother Nature and it's my job to make sure everything has a chance to grow and thrive."

De repente una voz dulce le habló a Jack. "Hola, Jack. Veo que has conocido a mis asistentes."

Jack miró en la lupa buscando la nueva voz. "Vaya, Jack, ya me estás mirando. Soy la tierra, y el aire; el sol y la lluvia. Soy la Madre Naturaleza y es mi trabajo asegurar de que todo tenga la oportunidad de crecer y prosperar."

Even green beans?" Jack asked.

"Even green beans, Jack. The plants work very hard and are very proud when their beans grow big and plump and are full of the taste of sunshine and rain.

"Maybe Grandma shouldn't pick them after they have done all that work," Jack said hopefully.

"But, Jack, all that work is the plants' way of giving you the gift of their beans. They want you to enjoy them. And your Grandma knows this. This is why she always says thank you as she picks them. And now that you know how those beans grew, why don't you go eat some?"

"¿Aún los ejotes?" preguntó Jack.

"Aún los ejotes, Jack. Las plantas trabajan muy duro y están orgullosas cuando sus ejotes crecen grandes y rollizos y están llenos del sabor del sol y de la lluvia.

Tal vez mi Abuela no los debiera cosechar después de todo ese trabajo," dijo Jack con esperanza.

"Pero, Jack, todo ese trabajo es la manera de las plantas regalarte sus ejotes. Quieren que los disfrutes. Y lo sabe tu Abuela. Es la razón que siempre da gracias en la cosecha. ¿Y ahora que sabes como se cultivan los ejotes, por qué no vayas adentro a comerlos?

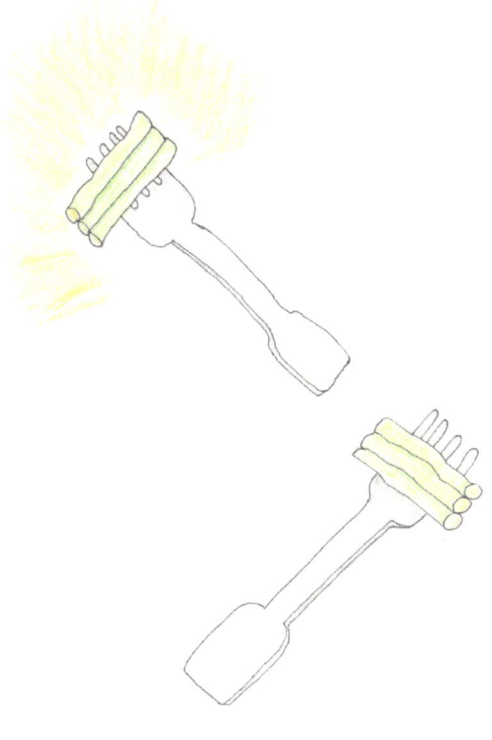

"Well, Jack, do you think you can eat a green bean now that you know more about them?" his Grandma asked when they were back at the table.

"Yeah, I guess," he said. "But only three!"

Grandma nodded. "Three will be just fine."

Jack ate three and he tasted the sunshine. He ate three more and he could taste the rain. Then he thought it would be nice to eat a bean for Clod, the worm wrangler, and one for Seed Nanny. So he did.

And when he looked at his plate, the beans were all gone!

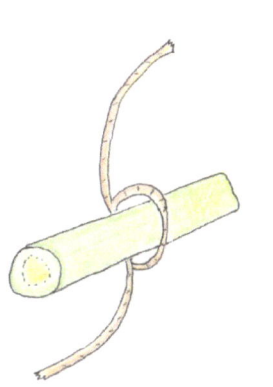

"¿Pues bien, Jack, piensas que puedes probar un ejote ahora que sabes más sobre ellos?" su Abuela preguntó cuando regresaban a la mesa.

"Tal vez sí, dijo, "¡Pero sólo tres!"

La Abuela asintió con la cabeza, "Comer tres está muy bien."

Jack comió tres ejotes y saboreó los rayos del sol. Comió tres más y pudo saborear la lluvia. Entonces pensó que sería amable comer un ejote por Clod, el vaquero gusano y uno por la Nana de Semillas. Y lo hizo.

¡Y cuando vio a su plato, se dio cuenta de que había comido todos los ejotes!

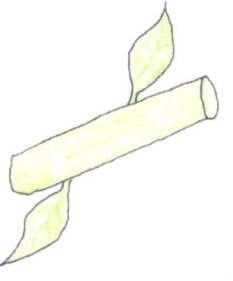

We Are What We Eat
Somos lo que Comemos
Foods & Animals of the Northwest
Comidas & Animales del Noroeste

Written & Illustrated by Kristy Stephens

An interactive story!
¡Una historia interactiva!

Follow along and participate with the actions of the native animals!
¡Sigan las acciones de los animales nativos!

The scampering Squirrel scurries to gather nuts and food for the long winter ahead.

La ardilla se anima a juntar las nueces y comida para el invierno largo que viene.

ACTION!
¡ACCIÓN!

Can you scurry to the next page like a squirrel?
¿Pueden apurarse a la próxima página como una ardilla?

The balanced Blue Heron stands patiently, waiting for its meal to swim by.

La Gran Garza Azul espera pacientemente, esperando que su comida nade delante de ella.

**ACTION!
¡ACCIÓN!**

Can you balance on one leg? How about the other?
¿Pueden mantener el equilibrio en un pie? Y ahora en el otro pie?

The bouncing Bunny eats as many leafy greens and vegetables as he can get his paws on!

¡El conejo corre y brinca para comer cuantas más hojas verdes y verduras pueda agarrar con sus patas!

**ACTION!
¡ACCIÓN!**

Show how you bounce like a bunny to the next page
Muestren como pueden brincar como un conejo a la próxima página

The buzzing Bee buzzes around to collect nectar from flowers to make honey.

La abeja hace zumbidos y zumba para recoger el néctar de las flores para hacer la miel.

ACTION!
¡ACCIÓN!

Can you buzz like a bee?
¿Pueden zumbar como una abeja?

Banana Slugs and busy Bugs may be small or slower, but they help create healthy soil for food and plants to grow.

Las babosas y Insectos ocupados puede que sean pequeños y más lentos, pero ayudan crear el suelo saludable para que crezcan la comida y las plantas.

ACTION! ¡ACCIÓN!

March like ants in a line to the next page
Marchen como las hormigas en una fila a la próxima página

The calm Cougar cub drinks milk to stay strong and loves plenty of rest and sleep to grow big.

El cachorro Puma bebe la leche tranquilamente para ser fuerte. Descansa bastante y duerme mucho para crecer grande.

ACTION! ¡ACCIÓN!

Can you cuddle and hug like the cougars?
¿Pueden abrazar como las Pumas?

The running Raccoon runs from here to there, looking for foods from all the different food groups.

El mapache se mueve rapidamente por todas partes, buscando los alimentos de todos los grupos de comida.

ACTION!
¡ACCIÓN!

How fast can you run like a raccoon to the next page?
¿Qúe tan rápido se pueden mover como el mapache a la próxima página?

The big Black Bear rolls on his back and eats handfuls of berries.

El gran Oso Negro se revuelca sobre su espalda y come un puño de moras.

ACTION! ¡ACCIÓN!

Can you name your favorite berry?
¿Pueden nombrar su mora favorita?

The frolicking Fawn can be found in farmers' fields, eating grains for extra energy.

El ciervo correteando se encuentra en los terrenos de los granjeros, comiendo los granos para más energía.

ACTION! ¡ACCIÓN!

Can you frolic like the fawn to the next page?
¿Pueden corretear como el cervato a la próxima página?

The Otter in the water loves to swim and float on his back among his many friends of the sea.

A la Nutria en el agua le encanta nadar y flotar en su espalda entre sus amigos del río.

**ACTION!
¡ACCIÓN!**

Can you hold your breath and pretend to swim through the air?
¿Pueden mantener la respiración y fingir de nadar en el aire?

Eat a variety of food to be strong, fast, and steady like the native animals! We all need a variety of foods from MyPlate.

¡Coma una variedad de alimentos para ser fuerte, rápido y tener energía constante al igual que los animales nativos! Todo el mundo necesita una variedad de comidas de MiPlato.

Make your plate a healthy plate!

¡Hacer su plato un plato saludable!

About the Authors and Illustrators

Toby and the Nine Grain Adventure

Audrey Andrews – Audrey Andrews is a freshman at Alliance Charter Academy and will attend Molalla High School for her sophomore year. She enjoys reading, writing, cooking, and sleeping. She aspires to be a famous chef.

Nikita Seledkov - Nikita Seledkov, 18, has lived in Clackamas County for over a decade. His passion for art flourished the more he practiced. Nikita likes to spend free time at home, drawing in his sketchbook. He wants to become an auto mechanic when he grows up because he loves cars and trucks.

Ruby's Special Pizza

Megan Cline - Normally, Megan Cline's stories are strictly for adult readers. However, when she heard about the Molalla Storywalk Project, she was up for the challenge of creating a story for young readers about an important topic. She was also excited to provide something fun and educational for the local community of Molalla. After pursuing career and educational opportunities in Portland, she returned to Molalla three years ago to put her Bachelor's Degree in English to work. In 2012, she launched *Starstruck Farmgirl Publishing*, an independent self-publishing label. She is currently working on publishing her first novel. Eventually, she hopes to expand her label to help other writers achieve their dreams.

Brie Riley – Illustrator Brie Riley graduates from Molalla High School this spring 2015. She has been a practicing artist since she was a small child, and created the artwork for *Ruby's Special Pizza* with the observation of her two young siblings.

Outdoor Fun (An I Spy Adventure)

Karen Graves – As a guide to the Molalla River Corridor and local author of the guide book *Lonely Trails*, Karen Graves has encouraged outdoor activity in the Molalla area for years. Her most recent book for kids, *What My Eyes Can Spy*, is a game book that sends folks through Yoder, Monitor, Mt. Angel, Silverton, Scott's Mills, Marquam, Molalla,

Colton, Springwater and Estacada. She is famous for her three, large toy bears that accompany her to promote outdoor adventures and tourism, and can often be found in the Molalla River Corridor on summer weekends and holidays.

Daisy – The Protector Dog Cares for Her Friends

Heather Nelson – Heather Nelson is a long time resident of the Mountain community, living in Rhododendron since the mid-1980s. Heather began writing children's stories for her grandchildren. One of their favorite stories was about *Daisy the Protector Dog*, a story focusing on love, kindness, friendship and protection from a dog's point of view. Heather published this story in 2012, so children everywhere can read about how dogs like to protect and care for their home and family. Other published works include *First Summer with Horses* and *Lost Family: FOUND!* She has four other children stories in progress at this time. The first of these new books is entitled, "Minerva's Maneuvers", about a little hyperactive girl and benefits of pet therapy. Heather is thrilled to have her story *Daisy the Protector Dog Cares for her Friends* selected for the Molalla StoryWalk.

Jack and the Beans

L. Lee Shaw - Inspired by a son who hated green beans, *Jack and the Beans* is the first children's story writer/publisher L. Lee Shaw has published. She has two prior novels, *Blood Will Tell...* and *Monster Child*. It also is the first time she has let her drawing skills out of the closet and shared publicly. L. Lee Shaw resides in Molalla.

We Are What We Eat

Kristy Stephens – Surrounded by nature, Kristy finds peace and inspiration for her illustration and writing, acrylic and oil canvas paintings, murals in nurseries and businesses, window painting, signs, graphic design and live painting events including wedding paintings. Kristy's window painting appear on businesses throughout Molalla. Her artistic career began in 2002 through family and friends but is growing as "word of mouth" reaches more people along with her internet presence. For more information about Kristy you can visit her website at www.paintingandmuralsbykristy.com or Facebook at www.facebook.com/artbykristy

www.ingramcontent.com/pod-product-compliance
Lightning Source LLC
LaVergne TN
LVHW071026070426
835507LV00002B/44